What people are saying about
AD/HD SUCCESS! Solutions for Boosting Self-Esteem: The Diary Method, Ages 7–17

"Kerin's understanding, borne of her many years of working in the field of AD/HD, has given her the ability to write a workbook that is an essential and comprehensive resource."

Roy J. Boorady, M.D.
Assistant Professor of Psychiatry, New York University School of Medicine
Director, Psychopharmacology Service, NYU Child Study Center

"Kerin, your workbook is amazing! It will not only be very useful and assist me during teacher/parent conferences, but it will definitely be a catalyst for change and inspire my students."

Ruthie Einhorn
Early Childhood Department, Moriah Day School, Englewood, NJ

"Wonderful...I enjoyed reading it; rather, was inspired. AD/HD SUCCESS! is sensitive, not overwhelming to kids, positive, and full of valuable suggestions."

Karen Kraskow, M.A., M.S.W.
Educational Therapist

"We are really looking forward to using this workbook with our daughter, who has learning issues. We know it will make a big difference."

Amy Lebovics
Bergen County, NJ

"This workbook was so helpful in developing inner values and goals with my elementary school population. For small or large group settings, the topics are very relevant to our student population and work as a great tool in initiating group topics. For teachers and counselors alike this is a wonderful tool to allow for a greater understanding of students."

J. Doshi, Counselor
Windsor Academy, West Patterson N.J.

"I love the workbook so much! I even keep it by my bed for reviewing it at night! I have been using simultaneously diary pages from different age groups as my daughter is very mature for age 10."

A parent from Brooklyn, NY

"I love the book so much that I took it to my daughter's school to show them just how helpful it has been to us to show them just what we are working on, and suggest they use such a workbook as an enhancement in the school system."

A parent from Bergen County, NJ.
Educational Therapist

AD/HD SUCCESS!
Solutions for Boosting Self-Esteem

The Diary Method

Ages 7-17

Kerin Bellak-Adams

From the "Growing with Love Series" at Loving Healing Press, Inc.

Author's website **www.ReachBeyondAdd.com**

Library of Congress Cataloging-in-Publication Data

Bellak-Adams, Kerin, 1959-
  AD/HD success! : solutions for boosting self-esteem the diary method for ages 7-17 / by Kerin Bellak-Adams.
      p. cm. -- (Growing with love series)
  Includes bibliographical references and index.
  ISBN-13: 978-1-61599-024-5 (trade paper : alk. paper)
  ISBN-10: 1-61599-024-0 (trade paper : alk. paper)
  1. Attention-deficit hyperactivity disorder--Treatment. 2. Self-esteem in adolescence. 3. Reinforcement (Psychology) I. Title.
  RJ506.H9B454 2011
  618.92'8589--dc22
                    2009052699

Published by
Loving Healing Press
5145 Pontiac Trail
Ann Arbor, MI 48105
USA

www.LovingHealing.com
info@LovingHealing.com

fax 734-663-6861
tollfree 888-761-6268

Distributed by Ingram Book Group (USA/Canada), New Leaf Distributing, Bertrams Books (UK), Hachette Group (EU).

Contents

SECTION THREE: FOR THE PARENTS

SECTION FOUR: THE SUCCESS STORIES

Dedication

I dedicate this book to my late father, Dr. Leopold Bellak, a renowned and legendary psychoanalyst, psychologist, professor, and consultant who authored 36 books and devoted endless amounts of energy to the development and integration of psychiatry, psychoanalysis, and psychology. Dr. Bellak had a dynamic influence on categorizing adult ADD as a genetically based disorder. His groundbreaking research on schizophrenia, as well as his creation of the Children's Apperception Test (the C.A.T., which has been translated into 18 languages), continues to provide a baseline for diagnosis and treatment of personality assessments worldwide. (For more information on Dr. Bellak and the C.A.T., please visit **www.CPSPublishingInc.com**.)

I also dedicate this book to my mother, Sonya Sorel Bellak, who was a great influence not only upon my father—as she helped him develop the C.A.T. and S.A.T. (Senior Apperception Test)—but also upon my younger sister and me. She imparted both the importance of helping others and the value of "giving"—standards that I try to live up to each day.

I also dedicate this book to my only child—my daughter, Dina Adams, whom I admire for her persistence, drive, and courage. Despite having auditory and learning challenges, she has miraculously achieved the highest levels of academic success throughout her years in school, as well as at Rutgers College of Nursing as an honors student.

I also dedicate this work to my late husband, Barry Adams, who lived each day as if it were his last, happily and fully, with contentment—a true role model for us all.

Finally, I dedicate this book to the research teams that have continued to work throughout the years in an effort to unlock the mysteries and find solutions in AD/HD treatment and diagnosis.

Acknowledgments

Thank you to my wonderful, understanding editor, Dawn Barnes, without whose ongoing patience I could not have completed this work; Rocky Buckley, for his direction as my original website and book designer; Bernice Golden, a dedicated and patient editor; Joe Schwab and Diane Turso, both sharp-eyed copyeditors; Vanessa Ploski from Mosaicology.com, my second website designer; Jennifer Bridges Brewer, my production consultant for design and layout; and Dan Connaghan, my current website designer. I would especially like to thank Judy Spiegel of Englewood, New Jersey, a parent whom I admire greatly and who initiated major changes in this book early on.

I thank Dr. Edward Hallowell, the renowned psychiatrist and author of *Driven to Distraction* as well as numerous other textbooks on AD/HD, who not only was kind enough to introduce me to numerous AD/HD professionals at my first ADDA (Attention Deficit Disorder Association) convention, but who also encouraged me to pursue my career as an AD/HD coach and speaker. His influence led to my becoming a professional certified coach through the International Coach Federation. I will always remember the story he told about his own teacher in early childhood, who took him aside and worked with him patiently and diligently. I am grateful to Dr. Hallowell for remarking to me that I am keeping my father's legacy alive in my own creative way.

I would also like to acknowledge the many dedicated parents out there—from the ones I have already met to the ones I hope to meet through the publication of this workbook—who make their children their number-one priority. To the parents who help their children to feel good about themselves by emphasizing their strengths, encouraging them to see their positives, and guiding them to develop interests and passions—I salute you!

SUCCESS DIARY POEM FOR KIDS!
by Kerin Bellak-Adams

I see I can do anything I really want to pay attention to.
I see I'm good and smart and okay after all.
I, like everyone, change and develop like leaves in the fall.
Using my imagination to learn new behaviors and attitudes can be fun,
just not as much fun as playing sports in the sun!
Getting to know myself is really pretty neat; I like to follow my own beat!
I love doing things that I'm good at, and I know I'll be a success as I go along.
These diary pages help me to see all that I do is great.
I know I will proceed into my future
at my very own rate!
I'm finding many days more enjoyable and fun;
I can see all the things I do right and feel good about myself most of the time
because now I feel like I am like a sculpture that is being polished as I continue to shine.

About This Resource

AD/HD SUCCESS! Solutions for Boosting Self-Esteem: The Diary Method Ages 7–17 is a simple, direct, and practical guide that will do the following: increase self-esteem, establish and influence positive attitudes and behaviors, and motivate each child/teenager to fulfill his or her individual potential. Insights and self-awareness as individuals as they interact with others will become a part of their consciousness. Along with this process, parents will get a fresh and insightful view of how their children feel about themselves, their child's level of motivation, and their self-esteem in social and academic environments. Open communication between parent and child will be more easily established as a baseline for future years of development. The Diary Method is easy to implement and is meant to be stress-free.

Benefits of the Diary Method

- ▸ **Children:** The primary benefit and outcome of using the Diary Pages is the boosting of self-esteem through the acknowledgement, reinforcement, and continued development of positive outlooks and behaviors.

- ▸ **Parents:** The responses to Diary prompts will give parents an inside view of just how their child is coping and feeling, and will provide clues to which coping methods do and do not work at home, in school, in after-school activities, and even during vacations! These prompts also provide an opportunity to create a closer bond between parents and their children and to develop open lines of communication in a stress-free, innovative manner.

- ▸ **Parents/Teachers:** This book is truly a workbook. **Parents** are strongly encouraged to bring the Diary Pages and the Home/School Daily Accountability Sheet to parent/teacher conferences! These pages encourage vital and open sharing of information and will ensure that both parties are on the same page.

- ▸ **Guidance Counselors and School Psychologists:** You can use these Diary Pages on a **one-to-one** basis or in a **group setting** throughout the year.

- ▸ **Time-Management Formula:** Time management is emphasized throughout the Diary Pages to encourage the development and reinforcement of routines and priorities, and to increase the consciousness of time.

- ▸ **Convenience:** This book is light and portable. You can even take it on trips and use the Diary Pages as a brush-up!

Why I Wrote This Book

As a former one-on-one teacher of children with ADD and AD/HD, I became acutely aware of the sensitivities of children and how easily they respond to positive reinforcement. Starting as early as first grade, self-esteem needs to be boosted and then maintained through the recognition of accomplishments. As a teacher, having witnessed amazing transformations and shifts in attitude with this continuous approach, I recognized that there is a void in schools—and sometimes in the home—much of the time in this crucial area. I realized that each and every student needs to be recognized as an individual with something special to offer both himself or herself and to others. This builds character. This approach can be the cornerstone for healthy and developmentally strong generations of children to come.

One day during my teaching years, I became curious if children understood the meaning of self-esteem. I asked a 10-year-old student if he knew what self-esteem was, and he replied excitably, "Yes, it's when I talk outside in the cold and steam comes out of my mouth!" This comment was one of the turning points that inspired me to write this book! It occurred to me that this was a largely unexplored area with children, and it was vital that it be addressed.

My objectives in this workbook are fourfold:

▸ My **main objective** lies in the definition of self-esteem as described by Richard L. Bednar and Scott R. Peterson in *Self-Esteem: Paradoxes and Innovations in Clinical Theory and Practice*: **[for people to] feel good about themselves when facing problems and anxieties so they deal with them rather than avoiding them.**[1] Through the use of the Diary Pages, children are offered a unique opportunity to establish self-esteem through positive reinforcement.

▸ My **second objective** is to **have children learn to acknowledge what they do right so they can feel much better about themselves over time, enabling them to be less self-conscious and more secure and courageous.** My hope is that this inner security will also encourage kids to verbalize their thoughts and feelings. I believe the assignments in "How High is My Self-Esteem?" and "If Your Kids Could Say What Is Really on Their Minds"—two key sections in this workbook—will propel this process of self-talk, leading to a positive self-image and providing kids the ability to endorse themselves for all that they do right, each and every day.

▸ My **third objective** is to **ensure that both parents and teachers give consistent messages to students.** So often, I hear parents voice their frustrations about the mixed messages that their children receive. One parent noted that while he was giving rewards to his 11-year-old with AD/HD for doing his homework every night, the teacher was also handing him delinquency slips for inappropriate behavior!

▸ The **fourth objective** is to **establish a more trusting and solid relationship between parents and their children/teens.** My wish is for parents to truly understand how they parent, realize what needs to be addressed with their children, and to help their children achieve a balanced perspective about themselves, emphasizing the importance of everything they do right and encouraging their aspirations.

---

[1] Richard L. Bednar and Scott R. Peterson, *Self-Esteem: Paradoxes and Innovations in Clinical Theory and Practice* (Washington, D.C.: American Psychological Association, 1995).

A Review of Self-Esteem and Positive Reinforcement

As children grow, they are under increasing pressure to learn more, to learn faster, and to keep up with ever-increasing competition. This pressure increases and is felt much more deeply when there is AD/HD involved. Thus, self-esteem has an even lesser chance to flourish. Children with AD/HD are often embarrassed at feeling and/or responding differently than their peers. Their "out of the box" thinking and acting can counteract any potential for feeling good. Add to the mix the stress of trying to keep up with others who may or may not have learning challenges—as well as the breakdown of the basic values of home life due to current divorce rates—and you have a situation that is not to be envied!

With increased stimuli from the outside environment and the emphasis on achieving instant gratification through technology, a connection to feelings is greatly compromised. With school systems emphasizing test results and percentiles, the basics of connecting to a child and what makes him feel better can get lost. Often, parents and/or teachers **unintentionally** neglect to recognize and verbalize the **positive efforts and behaviors** that children exhibit, especially in areas where they struggle the most. Too often, children receive attention primarily for negative behaviors alone—so how can self-esteem flourish? How can frustration tolerance develop and withstand the trials of life if self-esteem is not given a chance to be the springboard for their futures? Many times, parents are driven by fear and competition, and, as a result, create an atmosphere of skewed priorities. In addition, children are forced by technology's standards to keep busy and dependent on anything but themselves, leaving less room for a child to develop a true, positive sense of self.

Often, there are too few solutions—as schools evolve or do not evolve—to meet the growing needs of children and parents. The children pay the price for this, feeling different and misunderstood, and this affects their stress levels. I recall my daughter coming home one day while in second grade and remarking that she thought the school had forgotten that she was just a kid! She and her classmates were being kept busy and dependent on everything but themselves, pressuring them and diverting their attention and awareness away from their abilities to achieve on their own, naturally.

My personal observation is that teachers are under greater pressure than ever before to cover more material faster. This can put children who need more time and attention at a disadvantage. Continually emphasizing all the things that children do correctly will help children to **feel good about themselves**. It is important to keep in mind, as referenced in *Self-Esteem Revolutions in Children* by Thomas W. Phelan, Ph.D., that "people with higher self-esteem will try harder because they expect to succeed. People with lower self-esteem will give up sooner."[2] His book states that there may be a kind of overall global self-esteem, but there may also be specific self-esteem that occurs when people evaluate themselves in situations.[3] Children, for example, may have an *academic* self-esteem and a *social* self-esteem.

---

[2] Thomas W. Phelan, Ph.D., *Self-Esteem Revolutions in Children* (Glen Ellyn: Child Management, Inc., 1996), page 11.

[3] Phelan, *Self-Esteem Revolutions in Children*, page 66.

Self-esteem must be the bedrock, not only for those with AD/HD but also for those who experience other learning challenges. According to Dr. Phelan, there are four steps to boosting self-esteem: acknowledging strengths is the first step; doing positive activities with positive people is the second; the third is baby steps; and the fourth is the acknowledgement of the success![4] The Diary Pages integrate these steps.

Gradually, self-esteem changes the attitudes of children, encouraging greater sensitivity to themselves and others! Letting satisfaction and contentment develop—both academically and socially—leads to the fulfilling of potential and to reaching levels of fulfillment from within. Through the boosting of self-esteem, children are motivated to further explore their self-interests and discover their unique strengths.

This wonderful process starts with just highlighting the good! The joy is in the journey! Let's begin.

---

[4] Phelan, *Self-Esteem Revolutions in Children*, page 21.

SECTION ONE: GETTING STARTED

All About ADD and AD/HD: An Overview

Attention Deficit Disorder (ADD) is characterized by behavioral challenges that are caused by the blocking of common transmitters, such as serotonin and dopamine, which transmit messages from one neuron to another. In the brain of a child with ADD, these chemicals are often blocked, inhibiting the transmission of messages regarding everyday functions such as focus, organization, impulse control, awareness of time, anxiety regulation, and social skills. This is why the disorder is called "Attention Deficit." According to *Webster's Dictionary*, *dis* means "separation."[5] So *disorder* means "distanced from order." The same holds true for *disability*—"distanced from one's own true ability."

The good news is that with this "dis"order in daily life come strengths that are not all that common in people who do not have ADD. Often, one side of the brain is greatly enhanced with creativity and/or an acute ability to calculate and analyze challenging scientific or mathematical problems. Examples of dual capabilities along with their limitations have been identified in people including Albert Einstein, Dustin Hoffman, John Lennon, President Lincoln, and many more. This may be true for your children, who may achieve similar levels and become their own magnificent selves. One never knows!

Dr. Russell Barkley of Syracuse, New York, a psychiatrist and research professor of psychiatry at SUNY Upstate Medical University and a major contributor to ADD research, has stated along with other major contributors in the field that there are various forms of attention deficit disorder; however, all forms of ADD share common denominators. Each affects a person's lack of motivation in areas of study where there is little or no interest, such as in reading. People with ADD are also prone to losing items, short-term memory issues, delayed and/or prolonged stages of emotional growth, difficulty in following nonverbal and social cues, and limitations in verbal processing (which is what Albert Einstein suffered with all his life). Learning issues that accompany ADD often make life more complicated and drastically impede the development of self-esteem. ADD that does not come with learning challenges may create fewer issues, and ADD can even dissolve after the teenage years with some carry-over such as "perfectionism."

In **Attention Deficit Hyperactivity Disorder (AD/HD)**, hyperactivity is also involved. This means that there can be fidgeting of the hands, a constant need for movement, impulsivity (physical or verbal—such as blurting out thoughts without thinking about consequences or effects and interrupting others—all with good intentions), and physical and mental restlessness. These types of behaviors create feelings of being different and acting differently. Think of the activity for young children in which they try to put a circular block into a circle-shaped opening and a square block into a square-shaped opening, often needing several tries until they finally get it right. This process of elimination creates enormous frustration for the child with AD/HD, which may even carry-over into adult life! In addition to limitations that can be quite significant, AD/HD

---

[5] *Webster's New World Compact Office Dictionary* (New York: Wiley, 2003), page 186.

is quite often accompanied by gifts. While it may be difficult for children with AD/HD to stay in one place for any length of time or to hear themselves verbalize their thoughts until they understand them, they may possess tremendous intelligence, resourcefulness, mathematical capabilities, wonderful personalities of empathy and humor, and the ability to achieve a great many accomplishments that supersede those of the average individual.

Since negative feelings can be carried on from early childhood and adolescence, we want children/teens to become very attuned to their strengths as early on as possible. Not only will this confidence and sense of self act as a foundation of strength to handle life's challenges, but it will also enable them to accurately and fairly evaluate themselves despite childhood struggles.

Today, we know much more than ever before about ADD and AD/HD. Statistically, according to the Employment and Disability Institute at Cornell University in Ithaca, New York, approximately 4–6% of the U.S. population has AD/HD. This, however, does not include people who have either not revealed their AD/HD to their employer or who do not know that they have AD/HD. According to statistics from the International Dyslexia Association, one out of every eight children has learning challenges. There are some questions as to whether the increase in ADD and AD/HD diagnoses in children is due to the availability of drugs to treat their symptoms or reflects an actual increase in ADD and AD/HD. In 1979, Dr. Leopold Bellak chaired the first conference on Minimal Brain Dysfunction, the term for ADD before it was commonly known as ADD. At that time, health professionals were trying to identify parallels to other disorders that had some similarities and differences in relation to ADD.

The following excerpt from Dr. Leopold Bellak's book *Overload: The New Human Condition* provides perspective on just how intensely the feelings of overload have developed over the years. This society that we live in often lends itself to feelings of anxiousness, which sometimes is interpreted as having AD/HD.

> The swift changes in our world have also caused a decrease in the degree to which one can experience individuality and uniqueness—in the sense of self and self-esteem. If a child is constantly moved from one home to another, or from one school to another, when his father has been transferred from one city to another by his company (as is much more likely in contemporary times than a generation ago), he is hardly likely to develop a sound sense of self. Once upon a time, childhood experiences were acquired within the context of a family, which included usually not only father and mother but, typically, aunts, uncles, and grandparents. Among the middle class, a family doctor, the grocer, the butcher, and many other people constituted a rather permanent, personal, familiar environment. In today's world, the parents are often away from home; sometimes either because the father has to work far from home, or at other times because, being well-to-do, they take advantage of jet travel. Mothers, in all strata of society, frequently also work. Members of the family commonly live far apart, so that uncles, aunts, and grandparents are not around. It is a rare family that has a family doctor…Impermanence rather than permanence is the general key to life in our society.

School life is similarly structured. Children move in and out of neighborhoods and schools, and teachers rarely stay in one school for any length of time. A feeling of haste pervades the whole educational program. Children in high school particularly acquire a sense of being overwhelmed by their curriculum, by the tremendous number of innovations in all fields of human endeavor and by the tremendous speed of historical developments.

The speed at which changes are developing in our current society make it difficult to have the necessary feeling of being imbedded in a familiar context or of belonging. Having had so many changing experiences during the developmental process robs children of the feeling of identity that becomes internalized when the external environment is sufficiently stable.[6]

However, it's all in the attitudes of the parents. Albert Einstein's parents, for example, always made sure that Albert had his books before classes began. They encouraged him to try music and writing as a child, which probably led to his love for music. Just imagine what you could do for *your* child! Through this workbook, you'll discover just how much influence you can have.

How to Use This Workbook

For optimum use, based on feedback from parents and teachers who have field-tested the Diary Pages, each page should be used as an opportunity for exploration.

▸ Choose the Diary Page(s) that reflect the goals that you and your child/teen feel need the most attention. Make multiple copies of these pages and repeat them as often as necessary. *Once you and your child see consistent change and have satisfaction in the results, feel free to move on to another Diary Page.*

▸ Please have your child fill out the sections "How High Is My Self-Esteem?" and "If Your Kids Could Say What Is Really Their Minds" both *before* and *after* completing the Diary Pages; this will allow you to compare these sections to measure progress.

▸ For your convenience, PDF files of the Diary Pages, Home/School Daily Accountability Sheet, "How High Is My Self-Esteem?", "Assignments of a Different Kind", "Parent Self-Evaluation", and "If Your Kids Could Say What Is Really on Their Minds" sections are provided at **www.ReachBeyondADD.com** under the section "Books/Articles," enabling you to make as many copies as needed.

▸ The age ranges on the Diary Pages are there as a general guide; feel free to use any Diary Page that is appropriate for your child and/or situation.

▸ It is important to repeat and review the Diary Pages throughout the year for reinforcement and maintenance.

---

[6] Dr. Leopold Bellak, *Overload: The New Human Condition* (Human Sciences Press, 1975), pages 102–103.

- Use the Diary Pages and other sections repeatedly in *consecutive years* as your child/teen develops and for comparison.
- Emphasize the recognition of small efforts as being important.
- Practice my concept of Appreciation, Acknowledgement, and Action: be *aware* of your child's efforts, *acknowledge* them, and take an *action* to show it.

Remember, this workbook emphasizes what kids need most to feel good about themselves—results!

Notes for Parents

It is recommended that you keep the following points in mind before beginning this book:

- The Diary Pages are purposely written to allow for small steps to be taken to boost self-esteem. **Please don't allow your child to get overwhelmed.** If he/she shows disinterest, pick it up some other time or move to another section.
- Your attitude needs to be *nonjudgmental*. Show open satisfaction if your child accomplishes one or two of the actions on the page of your choice.
- Let these Diary Pages stimulate thinking and creativity. The development of **frustration tolerance** is a must!
- Ideally, this workbook should be used during a "quiet time," perhaps *before* bedtime, to encourage conversation and reflection. Build these Diary Pages into your schedule on a weekly basis.
- Encourage your child or teenager to think of his own acknowledgements, no matter how small they may appear.
- Encourage your child/teen to keep her own diary of what she does that helps her to feel good about herself throughout the year as well.
- Give extra copies of the Home/School Daily Accountability Sheet to teachers on a regular basis during the year. Bring completed pages to parent/teacher conferences for discussion and review completed pages with your child. If you communicate with your child's teacher via e-mail, you may also download the Accountability Sheet from **www.ReachBeyondADD.com** and e-mail it to the teacher.
- Have your child bring these forms into school and make sure to get them back each day! This builds accountability for your child and the teachers! Make sure to review the completed pages with your child.
- Consider having your son or daughter show their Diary Pages to their mental health professionals to demonstrate their growth and identify the areas they need to work on.
- The "For the Parents" section should be approached with an open mind and a willingness to grow. Repeat your section throughout the year and stay on your toes! Start your *own* diary!
- Explore your interests and/or passions and consider sharing them with—and including—your kids!

Notes for Teachers

Teachers, it is recommended that you encourage parents to work on the exercises with their children during the summer months. You will then be better equipped at the start of the school year to understand the areas where your students are in need of growth and positive reinforcement.

- ▶ The Diary Pages can be used as class work or homework. Make multiple copies of the Diary Pages and have your students fill them out either in the classroom or as homework. There are PDF files at **www.ReachBeyondADD.com** for the Diary Pages and the Home/School Daily Accountability Sheet for your convenience. You can also e-mail completed pages to parents on a regular basis.

- ▶ You can turn the Diary Pages into a game to see how many wonderful things a child/student can accomplish per week!

- ▶ Consider posting some Diary Pages in your classroom for your students and/or on Parents Night.

"The mediocre teacher tells. The good teacher explains. The superior teacher demonstrates. The great teacher inspires."
—William Arthur Ward

HOME/SCHOOL DAILY ACCOUNTABILITY SHEET

Student's Name _____

Teacher _____

Date _____

Dear _____,

Today, your child made an effort to continue working on controlling his/her behavior in class. Please follow through at home by reinforcing the importance of your child's efforts in the areas below that do NOT have checks.

Paid attention in class _____

Was polite _____

Raised hand instead of yelling out answer _____

Stayed focused _____

Was on time to class _____

Handed in homework signed by parent _____

Helped another student _____

Was enthusiastic in class while working with others _____

Worked hard on class work _____

Was focused on not breaking the rules _____

Handed in completed homework daily/weekly _____

Transitioned well from one class to another _____

Played nicely during recess _____

Kept a neat desk _____

Kept a neat locker _____

Arrived at school on time _____

For the Older Student:

Had a positive outlook about his or her interests _____

Did homework for extra credit _____

Was prepared for exams and reports _____

Was motivated to take AP courses in preparation for college _____

Please get in touch with me if you have any remarks or questions.

Sincerely,

Teacher Comments: _____

_____

_____

_____

_____

_____

_____

_____

_____

_____

_____

_____

SECTION TWO:
THE DIARY PAGES

A Note for Kids/Teens

*These Diary Pages were written just for **you**!* They are here to show **you** all the wonderful things you do right each day that you (and maybe no one else) have noticed! However, there will be days when you do not check as many actions as on other days. Do not get discouraged. This is normal! As long as you are aware of all the things you already do right, you will feel good about yourself. You may repeat these pages as often as you like. These are not tests! There are no right or wrong answers. How little or how much you write is up to **you**!

> ► Take your time! Answer the questions *at your own pace.* **Remember, these are not tests!**

> ► ***These Diary Pages are for you to realize all that you do right on your own, and to encourage you to develop even more in your behaviors and attitudes—both toward yourself and others around you!***

> ► Nobody is judging you! The more things you do right in a day, the better you will feel.

> ► Hold on to your Diary Pages so you can refer to them in the future.

NOTE: Please take a few minutes to fill out the "How High Is My Self-Esteem?" section on page 14 **before** you begin the Diary Pages and **again** *after* completing them. This will help you compare how you feel both before and after using the Diary Pages. Make sure you have copies of that section before beginning.

Feelings Rating Log

NOTE: On the bottom of *some* Diary Pages there is a "Feelings Rating" line. This is to help you identify how you feel that day. Using the numbers from 1 to 10 (see the number scale below), find the number that best describes how you feel about yourself *on that day.* For example: "10" means that you **feel great** about yourself today! "1" means that you **do *not* feel so great** about yourself today. Hopefully, as you work in this workbook, you will feel better and better about yourself!

Later on, you will be asked to see what number appeared most often! You can fill these sheets out during the year, then take a break and do them again at the end of the year to see how you've improved!

How High Is My Self-Esteem?

MAKE COPIES FIRST!

Directions for Kids: Before you begin the Diary Pages, please answer these questions by *circling the answer* that best describes how you feel or think! Be sure to make copies of this first before writing on it!

What is self-esteem? It's how good you feel about yourself—not because of what others say about you or what you think others think about you. It's how *you* feel about you inside. That's what really counts!

We want you to feel more and more comfortable with what you can say to your parents or others after circling these questions. Look at your answers, and then at the end of the year fill out this questionnaire again to see if, and how, you've changed!

1. Do you have enough courage to say to your parents: "Please help me pay attention better by looking at me when you speak."

    Always   Rarely   Never

2. Are you willing to ask your parents to let you know what to expect **before** they change your routine or move to a new activity?

    Always   Rarely   Never

3. Do you ever ask your parents if you can have a hug?

    Always   Rarely   Never

4. Do you ever feel like you want to say to your parents: "Please understand that *I am listening* to you, but sometimes I need things to be repeated!"

    Always   Rarely   Never

5. Do you ask your parents to let you know as quickly as they can how you are doing with your new efforts?

    Always   Rarely   Never

6. Can you ask them to say something calmly to you instead of yelling?

    Always   Rarely   Never

7. Do you ever ask your parents what they appreciate about you?

Always   Rarely   Never

8. How easily are your feelings hurt these days?

Very easily   Sometimes   Rarely

9. Do you keep your feelings to yourself?

Always   Rarely   Never

10. How long does it take you to get over being teased or criticized?

A long time   Some time   Not long

11. Do you find yourself wanting to get back at others who hurt you?

Usually   Sometimes   Rarely

12. Are you feeling better about making new friends?

Often   Somewhat   Not at all

13. Are you noticing when you feel bored in school and have trouble paying attention?

Usually   Sometimes   Rarely

14. Do you wish you had a close friend or more than one?

Often   Somewhat   Not at all

15. Do you ever feel like hurting others by screaming at them, but catch yourself and don't do that?

Usually   Sometimes   Rarely

16. What is one thing that you do or don't do that you would like to improve in and keep working on? Write down whatever comes to your mind.

_____

_____

THE DIARY PAGES

"If at first you don't succeed, do it like your mother told you!"
—Anonymous

Diary

Date _____

Check off any of these things that you did today!

_____ I brushed my teeth without being asked.

_____ I washed my hands before I came out of the bathroom.

_____ I ate my breakfast.

Today, I tried to be good in these ways:

1. _____

2. _____

Feelings Rating _____

Not Good		OK		Good		Great!	
①	③		⑤		⑦		⑩

"No man is useless while he has a friend."
—Robert Louis Stevenson

Diary

Suggested for Ages 7–8

Check off any of these things that you did today!

_____ I made sure that my lunch was packed for me to take to school.

_____ I was ready for the bus on time.

_____ I went to bed on time without whining or stalling (boy, did that feel different).

Today was a good day because:

1. _____

2. _____

"If there is anything a man can do well, I say let him do it. Give him a chance."
—Abraham Lincoln

Diary

Date _____

Check off any of these things that you did today!

_____ I shared the computer or television with my brother/sister or classmate.

_____ I came in for dinner as soon as I was told.

_____ I waited to say something to my parent until he/she was OFF the phone.

Today was a good day because:

1. _____

2. _____

Feelings Rating _____

Not Good	OK	Good	Great!
①	③	⑤	⑦	⑩

"The strong man is not the one who can show anger, but the one who can control his anger."
—Anonymous

Diary

Date _____

Did you manage to do any of these things today?

_____ I woke up when the alarm clock went off without going back to sleep!

_____ I quickly made my bed before going out of my room.

_____ I cleaned up part of my room.

Today, I am especially proud of myself because:

1. _____

2. _____

"God doesn't require us to succeed; he only requires that you try."
—Mother Teresa

Diary

Date _____

Check off any of these things that you did today!

_____ I thanked my teacher for the extra time he/she gave me on a test.

_____ At the end of the day, I took out my graded papers from my backpack and put them away where they belong.

_____ At night, I put out my clothes and even my backpack for school the next day.

I felt good today because:

1. _____

2. _____

3. _____

Feelings Rating _____

Not Good	OK	Good	Great!
1	3	5	7	10

"Every child is an artist. The problem is how to remain an artist once we grow up."
—Pablo Picasso

Diary

Date _____

Today was an especially nice day because:

_____ I handed my brother or sister the toys I thought he/she would like to play with.

_____ I didn't give my parent a hard time when he/she picked out the clothes he/she wanted me to wear.

Here are a few other reasons:

1. _____

2. _____

"Hating people because of their color is wrong. And it doesn't matter which color does the hating. It's just plain wrong."
—Muhammad Ali

Diary

Suggested for Ages 7–8

I had such a nice time with my parents at their friends' house!

_____ I didn't nag my parents that I was bored.

_____ I made myself useful by helping out.

Here are a few other reasons I feel happy about how I behaved today:

1. _____

2. _____

Feelings Rating _____

Not Good		OK	Good	Great!
①	③	⑤	⑦	⑩

"I wish people would love everybody else the way they love me. It would be a better world."
—Muhammad Ali

Diary

Date _____

My parents want to send me to a new school. I tried to act sensibly and:

_____ I asked them questions.

_____ I told them my feelings about the new school.

I'm OK with my feelings about this because:

1. _____

2. _____

3. _____

"What you pay attention to grows—so focus on the positive."
—Kerin Bellak-Adams

Diary

Date _____

I was in a bad mood when my parent woke me up this morning, but I still:

_____ took my medicines/vitamins.

_____ washed my face and combed my hair.

_____ pushed myself to get dressed.

I also:

1. _____

2. _____

Feelings Rating _____

Not Good	OK	Good	Great!	
①	③	⑤	⑦	⑩

"Even if you are on the right track, you'll get run over if you just sit there!"
—Will Rogers

Diary

Date _____

Suggested for Ages 9–10

Check off any of these things that you did today!

_____ I raised my hand in class to give an answer instead of shouting it out.

_____ I didn't tease anyone.

_____ I didn't laugh out loud when someone answered a question incorrectly.

_____ I didn't cheat by looking at my neighbor's work during a test.

_____ Even though I felt like having a tantrum when I had to do something in school that I didn't want to do, I took a breath and did it anyway.

Today, I tried harder to make sure I did things the right way in school by:

1. _____

2. _____

3. _____

"You can't hit a home run unless you step up to the plate. You can't catch a fish unless you put your line in the water. You can't reach your goals if you don't try."
—Kathy Seligman

Diary

Date _____

Check off any of these things that you did today!

_____ I reminded my parent that I needed to take my medicine(s) before leaving the house.

_____ I didn't nag my mom or dad after dinner.

_____ I said "Please" and "Thank you" to people.

_____ I waited my turn for my lunch while I was in line.

_____ I kept my place in line.

I paid extra attention when my parent said something to me today. Here is an example:

_____

_____

_____

_____

Feelings Rating _____

Not Good	OK	Good	Great!	
1	3	5	7	10

"If you have a positive attitude and constantly strive to give your best effort, eventually you will overcome your immediate problems and find you are ready for greater challenges."
—Pat Riley

Diary

Date _____

Check the things that you did today!

_____ I paid attention to what the teacher was saying and didn't talk to anyone sitting near me.

_____ I remembered to write my name on all of my homework.

_____ I didn't hog the ball during recess.

I really feel good about what I did in school today! Here are some examples:

1. _____

2. _____

3. _____

"You can do all things if you believe! Be of great courage."
—Anonymous

**Diary**

Date _____

Did you manage to do any of these things today? Check them off!

_____ When I came home, I ate a healthy snack (although those chips looked awfully good!).

_____ I made sure that I went to bed on time for a change!

_____ When I couldn't sleep, I put on my headphones so I wouldn't wake up anyone else.

Today, I can walk with my head held extra high because:

1. _____

2. _____

3. _____

*Feelings Rating*_____

Not Good	OK	Good	Great!
①	③	⑤	⑦	⑩

"I must respect the opinions of others even if I disagree with them."
—Herbert Henry Lehman

Diary

Date _____

Check off any of these things that you did in the last few days:

_____ I felt like cheating on a test, but I didn't even though I wasn't prepared.

_____ I started to organize my locker.

_____ I even checked my closet at home to make sure that everything was neat and easy to find.

_____ I'm not throwing my clothes on the floor like I used to. I even get them in the laundry basket sometimes!

Once in a while, even though I don't feel like it, I:

1. _____

2. _____

3. _____

"To be good you need to believe in what you're doing."
—Billy Crystal

Diary

Date _____

Did you manage to do any of these things today? Check them off!

_____ I paid attention to what the teacher was saying even when I was very bored.

_____ When I found I was talking too much to my friend, I moved my chair to a quieter place so I could concentrate on my work better.

_____ I stayed a few minutes after class to speak to the teacher to make sure I understood the homework.

I did something great today that I don't usually do:

1. _____

2. _____

3. _____

Feelings Rating _____

Not Good	OK	Good	Great!
1	3	5	7	10

"Every time you smile at someone it is an action of love, a gift to that person, a beautiful thing."
—Mother Teresa

Diary

Date _____

Check off the things you did today!

_____ I didn't whine or act like I'm the only kid in the family when I wanted some attention or something from my parent.

_____ I tried to do my homework when I was supposed to rather than watch TV or play video games.

_____ I helped clear off the table or dried the dishes.

I am starting to do some of these things on my own without being asked again and again:

1. _____

2. _____

3. _____

"All great change in America begins at the dinner table."
—Ronald Reagan

Date _____

Let's see, did you do any of these things today? Check them off.

_____   I invited a friend/classmate to my house for a playdate without having to be reminded by my parent.

_____   I invited a classmate over to my house to do homework together.

_____   I helped another kid with a problem he/she was having.

I'm making friends, and friends are important to me because:

1. _____

2. _____

3. _____

Feelings Rating _____

Not Good	OK	Good	Great!
①	③	⑤	⑦	⑩

"As we look ahead into the next century, leaders will be those who empower others."
—Bill Gates

Diary

Date _____

Check off any of these things that you did today!

_____ My friend seemed upset, so I tried to cheer him/her up.

_____ I studied in the library *instead* of going out to recess.

_____ I did an extra credit assignment.

_____ I was serious about doing my homework.

If I did any of the above things, which one made me feel the best inside?

1. _____

2. _____

3. _____

"Be nice to nerds. Chances are you'll end up working for one."
—Bill Gates

Diary

Date _____

The most important thing I have learned to do in school is to become more organized and stay that way:

_____ in my locker

_____ in my desk

_____ in my backpack

Here are some other ways I'm doing better with remembering things each day:

1. _____

2. _____

Feelings Rating _____

Not Good	OK	Good	Great!
①	③	⑤	⑦	⑩

"I really had a lot of dreams when I was a kid, and I think a great deal of that grew out of the fact that I had a chance to read a lot."
—Bill Gates

Diary

Date _____

Did you manage to do any of these today? Check them off!

_____ I didn't take anything out of my brother's or sister's room without asking *first*.

_____ I didn't complain when I had to do my brother's or sister's chore today.

_____ I helped my brother or sister find something that he/she lost.

_____ I made sure that my brother or sister had a snack after school when my mom or dad wasn't home yet from work.

Today, I treated my sister or brother nicely by:

1. _____

2. _____

3. _____

"Change will not come if we wait for some other person or some other time. We are the ones we've been waiting for. We are the change that we seek."
—*Barack Obama*

Check off any of these things that you did today!

_____ I wanted to yell or scream at someone today but told myself to calm down instead.

_____ I volunteered to hand out papers to my classmates or offered to go to the office for my teacher today.

_____ I quietly told a teacher or the principal when I saw someone being bullied.

_____ I tried to help someone in school find something that he/she lost.

_____ I didn't start crying when the kids yelled at me during recess because I couldn't play as well as the others. I just did the best I could and knew that was good enough, and reminded myself that it's only a game!

I don't always try to do something nice for someone else, but today I made an extra effort by:

1. _____

2. _____

*Feelings Rating*_____

Not Good	OK	Good	Great!
1	3	5	7	10

"If you're walking down the right path and you're willing to keep walking, eventually you'll make progress."
—Barack Obama

Diary

Date _____

Check off any of these things that you did today!

_____ I made sure to stick to my routine after school.

_____ At lunch, I cleaned up someone else's mess at the table.

_____ I cleared the dishes at home without complaining or whining.

_____ I tried to be on time for the bus so they wouldn't have to wait for me.

Tonight at dinnertime, I fooled everyone by:

_____

_____

_____

_____

_____

Feelings Rating _____

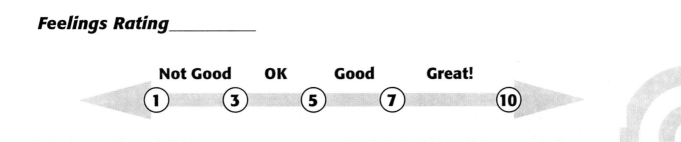

Not Good	OK	Good	Great!	
①	③	⑤	⑦	⑩

"Half a truth is often a great lie."
—Anonymous

Suggested for Ages 11–12

Did you do any of these things today? Check them off!

_____ I tried to help my brother or sister with homework. (Boy, I could think of other things I would have rather done!)

_____ I encouraged my parents to spend extra time with my brother or sister since I am told by my siblings that I get all the attention. (It doesn't feel that way!)

_____ I tried to help my brother or sister by explaining instructions to a game without asking for something in return (at least not today!).

Gee, what else did I do today? Did I appreciate nature or get a B on something I usually don't do well in?

_____

_____

_____

_____

"A positive attitude may not solve every problem but it makes solving any problem a more pleasant experience."
—*Anonymous*

Diary

Suggested for Ages 11–12

I had a lousy day at school, but when I came home, instead of shouting at the dog or doing something else naughty, I:

_____ washed my hands after playing outside.

_____ got myself a snack.

_____ looked at my schedule for the chores I was supposed to do.

Here are a few more things I did right:

_____

_____

_____

_____

_____

Feelings Rating_____

Not Good	OK	Good	Great!	
1	3	5	7	10

"Nothing is particularly hard if you break it down into small jobs."
—Henry Ford

Suggested for Ages 11–12

My day in school was a bit nerve-wracking! Usually I would go home and lie down, but today:

_____ I helped make my lunch for the next day.

_____ I took the dog for a walk without being asked.

_____ I made myself a healthy snack.

I also:

_____

_____

_____

_____

_____

"How wonderful it is that nobody need wait a single moment before starting to improve the world."
—Anne Frank

Diary

Date _____

Today was different because:

_____ I changed what I was wearing when my parent asked me to before leaving for school.

_____ I made sure to turn off the lights in the bathroom and my bedroom before going downstairs for breakfast.

_____ I put my clothes in the hamper.

I also behaved by:

_____

_____

_____

_____

Feelings Rating _____

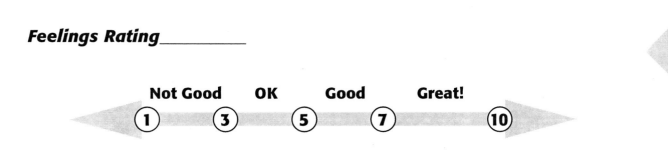

Not Good   OK   Good   Great!
1   3   5   7   10

"Imagination is more important than knowledge."
—Albert Einstein

Diary

Date _____

Today I pushed myself to work harder at:

_____ making a new friend.

_____ sitting with different friends at lunch.

_____ having my books ready for class and my homework on my desk, ready to hand in.

Let's see if I can think of anything else:

_____

_____

_____

_____

_____

"Don't give up five minutes before the miracle."
—A Twelve-Step Saying

Diary

Date _____

Check off what you observed yourself doing today:

_____ I took good care of my pet and/or its cage.

_____ I did all my homework where/when I am supposed to do it.

_____ I did my chores without complaining.

_____ I made sure I had my cell phone before leaving school.

_____ I didn't feed the dog under the dinner table!

What I pay attention to GROWS!

Lately, I have been paying *more attention* to the right things that I do each day. Here are some of them.

_____

_____

_____

_____

Feelings Rating _____

Not Good	OK	Good	Great!	
1	3	5	7	10

"Never be bullied into silence. Never allow yourself to be made a victim. Accept no one's definition of your life; define yourself."
—Harvey Fierstein

**Diary**

Suggested for Ages 11–12

Check off anything that someone else did FOR YOU lately!

_____ The bus driver waited an extra minute for me to get on the bus.

_____ A kid or teacher held a door open for me in school.

_____ My teacher took extra time after class to explain something I didn't understand during class or for homework.

_____ My parents remembered to say how much they love me or gave me a hug.

_____ My brother or sister said "Thank you" to me for a change!

_____ My mom, dad, and/or siblings came to my game.

I am noticing more of the nice things that others do for me:

_____

_____

_____

_____

_____

"Here is the test to find whether your mission on Earth is finished: if you're alive, it isn't."
—Richard Bachges

iary

Suggested for Ages 11–12

Check off any of these things you thought about the last few days!

_____ I saw what a good person I really am and how hard I try each day.

_____ Most of the time I stay organized at school, remembering to bring all my homework home.

_____ I realized all the good things I do for others!

_____ I appreciated all the little things around me, such as nature.

_____ I saw that I have important interests in my life—which I want to share with others! See? I have interests that I like to explore!

My interests are:

_____

_____

_____

This motivates me to keep trying because it really does pay!

Feelings Rating _____

Not Good	OK	Good	Great!	
①	③	⑤	⑦	⑩

"The art of living is more like wrestling than dancing."
—Marcus Aurelius

**iary**

Suggested for Ages 13–14

Check off what you did right today that made you feel proud.

_____ I'm not procrastinating (putting off) doing my homework for hours when I come home anymore!

_____ I am working to maintain the same schedule after school.

_____ I saw a kid crying, and I tried to help her/him or I went to the principal's office to get help.

FIRST THINGS FIRST! This is my routine.

_____

_____

_____

_____

_____

"Life is a long lesson in humility."
—James M. Barrie

Date _____

Suggested for Ages 13–14

This is **what I am going to do to make an effort to calm myself down on school nights**:

1. Set a time to get off the computer earlier: _____

2. Take a warm shower: _____

3. Set a time to turn off the light: _____

4. If I can't sleep, I won't make too much noise walking around, and I'll be extra careful not to break anything or make a mess! _____

5. Count my blessings:

_____

_____

Other things I can do:

_____

_____

_____

Feelings Rating _____

Not Good	**OK**	**Good**	**Great!**	
①	③	⑤	⑦	⑩

"It is important to foster individuality, for only the individual can produce the new ideas."
—Albert Einstein

Date _____

Suggested for Ages 13–14

Here is how I'm pushing to stay focused these days:

_____ I go to the library to do schoolwork when there is extra time during lunch.

_____ I break my work down into small parts so I don't feel so overwhelmed.

_____ I am trying to pay more attention to the time it takes me to finish my schoolwork.

I'm especially proud of myself because:

_____

_____

_____

_____

"A lie cannot live."
—Martin Luther King, Jr.

iary

Suggested for Ages 13–14

I am trying harder to:

_____ be prepared for quizzes and tests.

_____ start with the difficult work first.

_____ start my homework right after dinner instead of putting it off.

_____ set my watch to remind me when it is time to go to sleep.

_____ go to bed earlier.

What else?

_____

_____

_____

_____

Feelings Rating _____

| **Not Good** | | **OK** | | **Good** | | **Great!** | |
| 1 | 3 | 5 | 7 | 10 |

"Those who look only to the past or present are certain to miss the future."
—John F. Kennedy

**iary**

Suggested for Ages 13–14

These are areas to which I am trying to pay more attention:

_____   If I'm going to be late, I call home to let my parent know.

_____   I look forward to something at school.

_____   I try reading a book rather than being on the computer all the time.

Do I look forward to a certain part of my school day?

_____

_____

_____

_____

_____

"It doesn't matter how slowly you go—as long as you don't stop!"
—Confucius

iary

Suggested for Ages 13–14

Today was a great day because:

_____ I said what I meant instead of keeping it inside when it was the right thing to do [for example, saying no to someone].

_____ I looked at the bright side of the difficult times in school today.

_____ I went to a senior citizens' home to visit the residents.

_____ I worked on a school project with friends after school.

I feel great about myself and my challenges because without these I would never have:

_____

_____

_____

_____

_____

Feelings Rating _____

Not Good	OK	Good	Great!
①	③	⑤	⑦ ⑩

"In order to succeed, your desire for success should be greater than your fear of failure."
—Bill Cosby

Date _____

Suggested for Ages 13–14

Changes are on their way because:

_____   I like having friends over after school instead of being by myself.

_____   I make plans to study with friends after school.

_____   Sometimes I may ask my parent to help me with some homework or a problem I had with a kid at school.

Here are other things I like to do after school:

_____

_____

_____

_____

_____

"Look, I don't want to wax philosophic, but I will say that if you're alive you've got to flap your arms and legs, you've got to jump around a lot, for life is the very opposite of death, and therefore you must at very least think noisy and colorfully, or you're not alive."
—Mel Brooks

Date _____

No matter how hard something is for me in school:

_____ I don't feel sorry for myself. I think of what I can do that others can't do as well as I can!

_____ I try and try until I get it right.

_____ I don't give up on myself or what is important to me to accomplish.

Here are more things I do:

_____

_____

_____

_____

_____

Feelings Rating_____

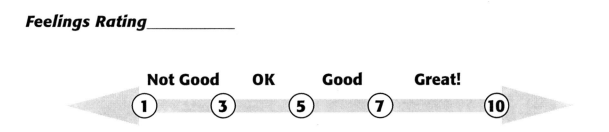

"If you want something done, ask a busy person to do it."
—Lucille Ball

Suggested for Ages 13–14

This is what I know kids like about me:

_____   my ability to play sports

_____   my ability to make others laugh

_____   my ability to get good grades

_____   my trustworthiness

Here are some more things I've noticed:

_____

_____

_____

_____

_____

"If you want to be respected by others, the great thing is to respect yourself. Only by that, only by self-respect will you compel others to respect you."
—Fyodor Dostoyevsky

**iary**

Suggested for Ages 13–14

I know my parents appreciate me and love me; I just wish that:

_____ they showed it more by reassuring me that everything will be ok.

_____ they would give me a hug sometimes.

_____ they would remind me what I good kid I am.

Here are more ideas:

_____

_____

_____

_____

_____

Feelings Rating _____

Not Good	OK	Good	Great!
①	③	⑤	⑦	⑩

"One of the things I learned the hard way was that it doesn't pay to get discouraged. Keeping busy and making optimism a way of life can restore your faith in yourself."
—Lucille Ball

Date _____

Suggested for Ages 15–17

Whenever I feel like I'm starting to panic, I try to remember to take a deep breath—and sometimes I even do! Here are some times when this happened recently:

_____   before taking a test in class

_____   when I thought I lost my homework

_____   when I got stuck on a problem in my work

_____   when I wasn't sure I knew the answer to a question the teacher asked of me

_____   when I wanted to show the teacher I knew more than someone else did

Here are some other times I noticed that I talked to myself in a positive way and I calmed myself down:

_____

_____

_____

_____

_____

"Attitude is more important than the past, than education, than money, than circumstances, than what people do or say. It is more important than appearance, giftedness, or skill."
—W. C. Fields

iary

Suggested for Ages 15–17

I've begun to notice that I get impatient or restless:

_____ when I don't understand something in class.

_____ when the teacher isn't talking slowly enough or isn't willing to repeat directions.

_____ when I'm waiting in line for something.

Now, I say something positive to myself, such as "Take it easy!" or:

_____

_____

_____

_____

_____

*Feelings Rating*_____

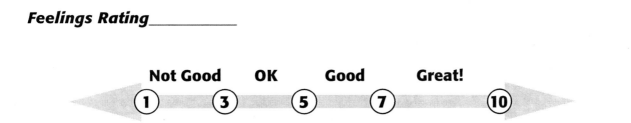

| Not Good | OK | Good | Great! | |
| 1 | 3 | 5 | 7 | 10 |

"You don't need fancy highbrow traditions or money to really learn. You just need people with the desire to better themselves."
—Adam Cooper and Bill Collage

**iary**

Suggested for Ages 15–17

I understand why having a little trouble with making or keeping friends or comprehending my work can sometimes be a POSITIVE thing!

_____ It gives me a chance to know things take time.

_____ I notice how long things sometimes take to work out, but they work out in the best way possible.

_____ I notice things about others that others might not (like who has a heart)!

_____ I even realize I understand things better when I see them rather than when I hear them.

Here are some other reasons why I'm grateful (for example, "I'm more sensitive to people's feelings"):

_____

_____

_____

_____

_____

"It ain't what they call you, it's what you answer to."
—W. C. Fields

iary

Today I felt good about doing something that I don't usually do.

_____   I let my friend speak up first during a disagreement.

_____   Even though I was angry with a friend, I decided not to say what was on my mind.

_____   I didn't walk away in disgust from my friend. We worked it out together.

Here are some other examples where I held my tongue!

_____

_____

_____

_____

_____

_____

Feelings Rating_____

Not Good	OK	Good	Great!
1	3	5	7	10

"Reach high, for stars lie hidden in your soul. Dream deep, for every dream precedes the goal."
—Ralph Vaull Starr

iary

Suggested for Ages 15–17

Here is what I seem to appreciate most about myself these days:

_____ my personality

_____ my appearance

_____ my sense of humor

_____ how well I do in class in a particular subject

_____ how well I do in sports

_____ my attitude toward myself; I take myself more seriously now

Here are some other things I like about myself or do well in:

_____

_____

_____

_____

_____

"Nothing can stop the man with the right mental attitude from achieving his goal; nothing on earth can help the man with the wrong mental attitude."
—Thomas Jefferson

iary

Suggested for Ages 15–17

Here is what I think I have an easy time with:

_____ listening well

_____ speaking my mind when it counts

_____ paying attention in class

_____ trying to be polite

_____ trying to show appreciation to others

_____ trying to stay positive about my future

_____ I don't give up even when I'm exhausted; I take a break and then go back to my work

Other things I do well:

_____

_____

_____

Feelings Rating_____

Not Good   OK   Good   Great!

①   ③   ⑤   ⑦   ⑩

"Follow your bliss and the universe will open doors for you where there were only walls."
—Joseph Campbell

iary

Suggested for Ages 15–17

I want to explore these interests of mine further:

_____ art

_____ science

_____ history

_____ sports

_____ animals

_____ helping the elderly

_____ reading to children (especially in hospitals)

Here are some other areas I am interested in:

_____

_____

_____

_____

_____

"I couldn't wait for success, so I went ahead without it."
—Jonathan Winters

Date _____

If I could wish upon a star for things to change in me, the changes would be:

_____ to have more patience with myself

_____ to offer someone a hug or a pat on the back once in a while if I think they need it

_____ to stand up straight, which shows I like myself

_____ not to hang out with kids that get into trouble

Any others?

_____

_____

_____

_____

_____

Feelings Rating _____

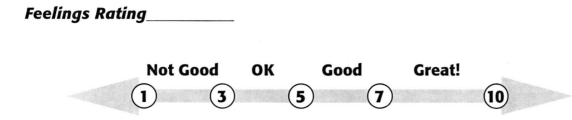

Not Good   OK   Good   Great!
1   3   5   7   10

"A man is but the product of his thoughts. What he thinks, he becomes."
—Mohandas Gandhi

iary

Suggested for Ages 15–17

I feel more comfortable:

_____ with one friend.

_____ in groups.

_____ when I'm alone.

Here are the reasons why I feel this way:

_____

_____

_____

_____

_____

"Action expresses priorities."
—Mohandas Gandhi

iary

Suggested for Ages 15–17

This is what I think is missing in my life:

_____ a few close friends

_____ one close friend

_____ a way to describe my feelings to my parents

_____ a real interest in others

_____ finding something I love to do and look forward to

_____ a way to express what I am thinking or feeling

_____ fun

_____ imagination

Here are some other things:

_____

_____

_____

Feelings Rating_____

	Not Good	OK	Good	Great!	
	1	3	5	7	10

"Focusing your life solely on making a buck shows a certain poverty of ambition. It asks too little of yourself. Because it's only when you hitch your wagon to something larger then yourself that you realize your true potential."
—*Barack Obama*

iary

Suggested for Ages 15–17

I know that most of my teachers feel good about how I work in school because:

_____ I don't give up trying to understand what is difficult.

_____ I ask questions if I don't understand something.

_____ I try to be helpful to others.

I also try to:

_____

_____

_____

_____

_____

"Try not to become a man of success but rather try to become a man of value."
—Albert Einstein

iary

Suggested for Ages 15–17

Here are some ways I am exploring what I like to do each day:

_____ I'm reading more.

_____ I'm painting.

_____ I'm learning an instrument.

_____ I'm raising money for my favorite charity.

Here are some other things:

_____

_____

_____

_____

_____

Feelings Rating_____

Not Good	OK	Good	Great!	
1	3	5	7	10

"If you have no confidence in self, you are twice defeated in the race of life. With confidence, you have won even before you have started."
—Marcus Garvey

Feelings Rating Tally

Directions: Let's count up the "Feelings Rating" numbers one (1) to ten (10) to see just how often they appear on your completed Diary Pages. Remember, count all your pages—even those that were repeated.

On the lines below, write down the tally for each Feelings Rating number. For example: go through your Diary Pages and count how many times you chose the number "1" in your Feelings Rating. If you chose the number "1" ten times, then you would write the number "10" on the line below next to the number "1."

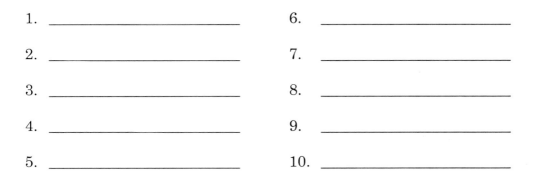

1. _____   6. _____

2. _____   7. _____

3. _____   8. _____

4. _____   9. _____

5. _____   10. _____

Based on your tally above, what number appears *most often* in your Feelings Rating? _____

This tells me just how often I am beginning to feel better about myself as I've become more aware of all that I do right!

I realize some positive things about myself as a result of some of my challenges that others may not be aware of:

_____

_____

_____

_____

Diary

Assignments of a Different Kind

MAKE COPIES FIRST!

For *best results*, please complete these assignments every day **for two weeks** and write down your answers **in as much detail as possible**.

Assignment #1

1. Give specific examples of ways that *YOU gave to others* in school or at home:

2. Write down ways that *others gave to YOU* in school or at home:

3. How *did you* NOT *cause worry or stress to your parents, teachers or friends*?

Assignment #2

1. Describe how it feels to look in the mirror and give yourself a hug.

2. Write yourself a friendship card as if it were from someone else. What nice things would it say?

3. Write about how much better you feel about yourself after completing this Diary.

Diary

Date _____

Here are some blank lines for you to write whatever you want. You may want to write down things about yourself that you notice have improved over the past year, as well as things that make you say YES to yourself! Make copies of this page before writing, and use them to start your own Diary!

_____

_____

_____

_____

_____

_____

_____

_____

_____

_____

_____

_____

_____

_____

_____

_____

SECTION THREE:
FOR THE PARENTS

A Parent's Gift
by Kerin Bellak-Adams

Show all children the beauty they have inside.
Let this give them a quiet sense of pride.

Allow this self-awareness to be a safe place from within.
Growth will stem from it and pain can heal.

All the layers will begin to peel.

Teach your teens to dream.
Encourage their imagination to soar.
Let them experience and develop a passion
while embracing themselves for who they really are;
this will enable them to go very far.

Inner strength will blossom
and a happier life they will find;
all they truly need is patience and some extra time.
Your look into their eyes will say everything will work out just fine!

Parent Self-Evaluation

MAKE COPIES FIRST!

Directions: *Parents:* Please answer the following questions thoroughly and honestly. Repeat this self-evaluation frequently throughout the year and see how your answers change. This process will help you evaluate *your progress* with your parenting skills. This is a good tune-up and *maintenance* plan of action!

1. How did I build on one of my child's **strengths** today? Did I recognize that he or she followed his or her routine?

   _____

   _____

2. Did I encourage my child to focus on **his or her interests** today? How?

   _____

   _____

3. Instead of screaming, did I ask myself the question: **"How important is this?"** Did I pick my battles? How?

   _____

   _____

4. When I had other things on my mind, when did I pull back and make my child **my first priority**?

   _____

   _____

5. When did I display respect or give a hug, a smile, or a wink while looking at my son or daughter **in the eye**?

   _____

   _____

6. How have I practiced using a **sense of humor** lately?

   _____

   _____

7. How did I surprise myself by **behaving differently** with my child or teen this week? Did I do something that allowed me to step out of my comfort zone? Would I try doing it again?

_____

_____

8. Did I use imagination, fairness, **patience**, impulse control, speech control, or anything else that made me feel good about myself and helped my child feel more secure?

_____

_____

9. What are three ways that I demonstrated my expectations of my child's responsibilities **without engaging in power struggles**?

_____

_____

10. Did I encourage my child or teen to be open with me today? Did I suggest games or activities that utilize **cooperation** rather than elimination?

_____

_____

11. Did I utilize **time-out**? Was it for my child or me? Let's get real! Was there something else I could have done instead?

_____

_____

12. Am I getting into the habit of establishing and reinforcing **routines** for my child?

_____

_____

13. Am I maintaining **boundaries** on a regular basis?

_____

_____

14. Are we as parents both **on the same page** with our expectations for our children? If not, what are we doing about it? Are we giving mixed messages?

_____

_____

15. Are we both **sharing the responsibilities** for our children and putting them first?

_____

_____

16. Am I remembering to **make sure that my child takes his or her medicine** every day?

_____

_____

17. Am I remembering **not to take myself too seriously** all the time?

_____

_____

18. Am I making **myself a priority** some of the time?

_____

_____

19. Am I encouraging my son/daughter to feel that it is **safe to talk** to me? How?

_____

_____

20. Am I being a good role model by **showing respect** toward my spouse or significant other?

_____

_____

21. Am I **not rushing** my child to do more than what he or she can, and expecting progress rather than perfection?

_____

_____

22. Am I **controlling** my own anxiety so it doesn't affect my children?

_____

_____

23. Am I providing my child with **books** before the next semester so he or she can get a **head start**?

_____

_____

24. Do I encourage my child to understand or see how I **advocate** for him or her in school?

_____

_____

25. Are my spouse and I **taking turns going to parent/teacher conferences**?

_____

_____

26. Are we **expressing gratitude** to our child's teacher at parent/teacher conferences?

_____

_____

27. Are we thinking about which schools will be **best for our child in the future**? Do we let our children/teens have enough of a say in the matter?

_____

_____

28. Do I make sure that both my partner and I **acknowledge** our child/teenager for who he is today, rather than waiting until he is grown up?

_____

_____

29. Do I break things down into **less overwhelming terms** when trying to explain actions that need to take place to fulfill a goal at home, school, or even on vacation?

_____

_____

30. Do I find myself usually judging my child rather than giving him or her the **benefit of the doubt?**

_____

_____

31. Do I emphasize the **positive** side of social or academic situations to my children as they are struggling through them? How often am I a **reassuring** parent?

_____

_____

32. How often do I make a point of **sharing** my interests with my child?

_____

_____

33. When was the last time we told our son/daughter just how much of a **difference** he/she makes in our lives? Can we remind each other to do this from time to time?

_____

_____

34. On a scale of 1–10, how would I rate my ability to serve as a **good role model** for my child?_____

_____

_____

35. What will my daughter/son **remember the most** about time we spent together?

_____

_____

36. Do either of us as parents encourage our children to pursue their dreams and encourage them to **be who they are?**

_____

_____

37. Do we tell our children that it is **okay to be different?**

_____

_____

PARENT SELF-TALK COPING STRATEGIES

Reward direction; progress, not perfection, is what counts.

The *joy* is in the journey.

Imagination can be the salvation. (This is what Albert Einstein felt!)

Keep it *simple*, sweetie.

Endorse, endorse.

What you pay attention to will *grow*!

Passion is the sanction!

If Your Kids Could Say What Is Really on Their Minds

Directions:

- Read each item. Have your child put a **check** next to the items that he/she can relate to.

- Make several copies of this form and repeat this activity throughout the year to measure just how easier it becomes for your child/teen to verbalize his/her thoughts.

1. **"Please HELP ME TO FOCUS."** Teach me with a "hands-on" approach rather than telling me! _____

2. **"I NEED TO KNOW WHAT TO EXPECT *NEXT."*** Please give me a chance for quiet time just to relax. If you make changes to my routine, could you please let me know a little ahead of time? I hate change! ____

3. **"WAIT FOR ME. I will get it; it just takes me a little longer."** I'm still trying to figure this thing out. Please don't rush me—I will get confused and want to quit. Can we come back to this one later? ___

4. **"PLEASE GIVE ME DIRECTIONS ONE STEP AT A TIME."** Could you encourage me to tell you what I think you said? ___

5. **"Please remind me to set my watch. YOU KNOW I DON'T HAVE SUCH A GREAT SENSE OF TIME."** I need short periods of time to study. Can I take breaks in between? ___

6. **"PLEASE TELL ME THAT MY PROGRESS IS GOOD ENOUGH."** Do I have to be perfect? ___

7. **"PLEASE REMIND ME OF ALL MY GOOD POINTS WHEN I'M HAVING A BAD DAY!"** ___

8. **"PRACTICE** what you preach!" _____

SECTION FOUR:
THE SUCCESS STORIES

The Student Success Stories

Below are some success stories of children's behaviors and attitudes that I experienced in school as a teacher. As a paraprofessional in a local elementary school in Bergen County, New Jersey, I witnessed the constant endorsement and acknowledgment of small accomplishments, which resulted in remarkably improved efforts and shifts in attitude and behavior. I have seen profound change in children who were previously unwilling to be quiet, antsy and needing extra attention, refusing to do homework or participate in outdoor fun activities for any length of time, and exhibiting many other common forms of everyday problematic behavior.

A 5th Grader

I had a student who refused to sign out when going to the bathroom. He would continuously ask if quizzes had been marked. He talked a lot in class and generally exhibited behavior that showed that his parents encouraged him to feel special and superior to the other children. Once, when he tripped outside over something small, he said, "Could I go to the nurse's office? I have an audition today after school." I would comment quietly when he acted out, saying, "I know you can act the way I would expect; I have lots of confidence in you." Slowly, he evolved into a different type of child, and the transformation was amazing. He would sign the book before going to the bathroom. He even removed himself from a noisy section of the room and sat quietly in a corner to complete his work in class! He would volunteer to help others and hand out papers for the teacher. He would wait to speak until teachers had finished speaking to each other.

A 7th Grader

A child in 7th grade came up to me with tears in his eyes, saying that a group of kids were bullying him. He said that his uncle always encouraged him to beat them up. I said that would not be acceptable behavior, but he kept repeating it and throwing sticks at them. He said they would not let him join the softball game because he was short. While tears streamed down his face, I reminded him of a speech I had heard at the school on bullying. The speaker said, "Hurt people hurt others." I explained that this means that kids are mean because they are in pain, and their teasing had nothing to do with him at all. They just needed someone to focus on to distract themselves from their pain.

He listened carefully as we strolled during recess. I explained that if he just walked away when they called him short, they would see that they couldn't get a reaction out of him and would lose interest. I reminded him that he was not the only one who was teased, and I reminded him of the time when there was an assembly on bullying, where children stood in line to tell their stories about being made fun of and how it made them feel. I told him the most important thing is to connect with the heart and not to try to get back at a group. He looked at me and then walked away. Two weeks passed before I saw this child again. He pointed to me and said, "I remember you; you're the one that said 'Hurt people hurt … people.'" I replied, "Yes, oh, so you remember?" He said that the group did not bother him anymore. I asked him, "What do you think might have changed?" He said he didn't know, but that it didn't happen anymore. I replied that it was probably his attitude that they picked up on. I walked away with a smile.

Another 5th Grader

For the sake of anonymity, I will call this child "George." He has many siblings and a twin. George has learning issues and emotional issues, often spacing out and "thinking all the time," as he would say. He would leave playtime to stand by the door until recess was over. Sometimes he would hit his head on the desk when he didn't get a question right in class, often being on the verge of tears. Once I started paying attention to him and encouraging him to talk things out with me, things improved. I started to see him reaching out to other teachers. I would always remind him of how well he did in math, and I suggested that he should try helping others who were less capable. I told him that I expected him to give his assignments a try even when he didn't feel like it, or to do his homework during classroom time. When the teachers saw him making an effort, they called on him more frequently in class. I gave him special attention during recess and in class, and he became happier. He opened up easily, and this made it much easier to help him with his issues. I always reminded him how smart he is, especially in math, and that left-handed people are very often the smartest ones.

George and his twin are almost too difficult to tell apart. Once, when I told him I could finally tell them apart, he asked me why. I replied, "Because when people get to know the two of you, they can see a big difference." He thought this was because he had a tiny growth on his nose that helped me tell them apart. Now George smiles instead of cries.

Another 5th Grader, My Own Student

In the beginning of the school year, this 5th grader, classified with ADD, picked at his fingers and didn't transition well. He generally kept to himself, not knowing how to socialize. When he would pick at his fingers at his desk, I would tell him quietly to try to relax, and everything would be fine. I helped him with his work and, months later, I encouraged him to try to sit with his friend rather than alone, on the same bench as the other classmates. Although his reactions were slightly out of sync with the others in class, he did remain friends with this particular child, and I continued to encourage them to have playdates, which they did.

He eventually gained enough social skills to look at his friend with a gleam in his eye and, after much encouragement, to participate in playing with his classmates outside, rather than just observing them. He was no longer afraid or nervous. He had blossomed, and the Special Needs Director told me she felt like crying, for he was really on his way.

Famous People With AD/HD or AD/HD-type Symptoms

Albert Einstein

Einstein didn't begin to speak until after the age of two, which made his parents worry that he was slow and ignorant. Throughout his life, Einstein suffered from *ecolalia*, causing him to repeat phrases to himself, often two or three times. Others labeled him as "almost backwards," and the family maid dubbed him "the dopey one." Whenever he had something to say, he would try it out on himself first, whispering it softly until it sounded good enough to pronounce aloud. He had such difficulty with language that those around him feared he would never learn! Ironically, his speech development allowed him the freedom to observe space and time with a sense of wonder. He developed tremendous visual capacities that enabled him to create his theories and develop his concept of relativity. Einstein believed that these capacities allowed him to observe with wonder the everyday phenomena that others took for granted.[7]

Einstein's parents were patient, understanding, and one step ahead, as they made sure that he received his books for classes early so he would have a head start on the subjects to be taught. However, he was arrogant, had difficulty tolerating authority, and often had trouble with his teachers. After dropping out of high school, he attended the Zurich Polytechnic Institute (where he met his wife-to-be, Mileva Maric). Even though he graduated, Einstein had trouble finding work; due to his difficult reputation while at the Institute, professors were unwilling to write him recommendation letters.[8]

Nevertheless, Einstein's perseverance would serve him well throughout his life in all respects. He married Mileva and flourished in his family life. As an adult, Einstein retained the intuition and the awe of a child. He envisioned that he would one day win the Nobel Prize—which he did, in 1921, for Physics.[9]

John Lennon

John Lennon had a history of doing poorly during all of his school years until high school, when his parents transferred him to the Liverpool College of Art. His passion for music no doubt overcame any lack of self-esteem he might have experienced. It could be said that he became both professionally and romantically successful and fulfilled. He made a difference.

Dustin Hoffman

Dustin Hoffman, known as "Dustie" as a youngster, attended a Jewish high school but didn't feel like he belonged there. He enrolled in an African American high school and loved it—he was the only Jew, and he enjoyed being different. One day, in dismay and fear, he asked a friend what he could do for a living, as he was used to doing very poorly in school. His friend suggested acting since that would be the only career where he couldn't be fired. Hoffman was able to build a successful career, develop a close and

---

[7, 8, 9] Walter Isaacson, *Einstein: His Life and Universe* (New York: Simon & Schuster, 2007).

wonderful long-term marriage, and have two wonderful children—and overcome his low self-esteem.[10]

Other Famous People with AD/HD or Similarities

Michael Phelps is a true athlete who won eight gold medals for swimming in the Beijing 2008 Summer Olympics. He suffered with AD/HD all throughout school, but he never lost sight of his passion! He used his ability to hyperfocus to make his life work!

Winston Churchill (for whom the Churchill School and Center in New York City for children with learning disabilities was named); Helen Keller; Jet Blue Airways CEO David Neeleman; Thomas Edison; Scottish physicist James Maxwell; Isaac Newton; and countless others all suffered with AD/HD-type symptoms, yet they had a vision ... and made a difference!

Share Your Success Stories!

As a speaker, I share many stories of parents, teachers, and children facing the challenges of AD/HD with my audiences. I would love to hear about your own success stories, especially the funny or frustrating ones. We're all in this together, and we can all draw courage and inspiration from one another.

Please feel free to e-mail your stories to me at **reachbeyondadd@aol.com**. You may write anonymously or with just your first name if you wish; it would be helpful to know your location, but it is not essential.

The journey to AD/HD success is a demanding but rewarding one. I look forward to taking it with you!

Kevin Bellet-Adams

---

[10] *Inside the Actor's Studio: A TV Interview with Dustin Hoffman*, 2006.

Bibliography

Bednar, Richard L. and Scott R. Peterson. *Self-Esteem: Paradoxes and Innovations in Clinical Theory and Practice.* Washington, D.C.: American Psychological Association, 1995.

Bellak, Dr. Leopold. *Overload: The New Human Condition.* New York: Human Sciences Press, 1975.

Bellak, Dr. Leopold. *Psychiatric Aspects of Minimal Brain Dysfunction.* New York: Grune & Stratton, 1979.

Inside the Actor's Studio: A TV Interview with Dustin Hoffman, 2006.

Isaacson, Walter. *Einstein: His Life and Universe.* New York: Simon and Schuster, 2007.

Phelan, Thomas W. *Self-Esteem Revolutions in Children.* Glen Ellyn: Child Management Inc., 1996.

Webster's New World Compact Office Dictionary. New York: Wiley, 2003.

Recommended Reading

For Teachers and Professionals

The ADD Nutrition Solution by Marcia Zimmerman, C.N. (Holt, 1999)

Adult ADD by Dr. David Sudderth and Dr. Joseph Kandel (Three Rivers Press, 1996)

Attention Deficit in Adults, 4th Edition by Lynn Weiss, Ph.D. (Taylor Trade Publishing, 2005)

Driven to Distraction by Dr. Edward Hallowell and Dr. John Ratey (Touchstone, 1995)

Emotional Intelligence by Daniel Goleman (Bantam Books, 2005)

For Parents

Answers to Distraction by Dr. Edward Hallowell and Dr. John Ratey (Bantam Books, 1996)

Non-Verbal Learning Disabilities at Home by Pamela B. Tanguay (Jessica Kingsley Publishers, 2001)

Only a Mother Could Love Him by Ben Polis (Ballantine Books, 2004)

Overcoming Dyslexia by Sally Shaywitz, M.D. (Vintage, 2005)

Ready or Not, Here Life Comes by Mel Levine (Simon & Schuster, 2005)

About the Author

Kerin Bellak-Adams is a highly respected expert in AD/HD and an authority on building self-esteem in children and adults. She is a certified coach with the prestigious International Coaching Federation and a member of the executive board of C.H.A.D.D. (Children and Adults With Attention Deficit/Hyperactivity Disorder) of Bergen County, New Jersey. Kerin is often compared to her father, the late Dr. Leopold Bellak, an internationally renowned psychoanalyst and pioneer in adult ADD and schizophrenia. Her practical and unique approach to helping others has earned her the respect of such experts as Dr. Edward Hallowell, respected psychiatrist and former professor at Harvard Medical School; the psychiatrists at the New York University Child Study Team; and Dr. Stanley Greenspan, world-renowned psychiatrist, author, and expert in dyslexia.

A sought-after speaker and writer, Kerin has addressed parents and special education teachers on self-esteem and time management; she now addresses business executives and their companies as a motivational/educational speaker on time management and organizational skills. Kerin has worked as a one-on-one teacher of children with ADD and AD/HD and has plenty of first-hand experience as the mother of a grown daughter with learning challenges.

Kerin is a graduate of Hofstra University with a bachelor of arts degree in liberal arts, with a focus on social sciences. She is also a graduate of the American Coaching Institute (the pioneering school for coaching adults with ADD) and a graduate of Fast Track Coaching. She has been accepted into the School of Social Work of Yeshiva University, New York City, and The Institute of Training in Psychoanalysis in New Jersey.

Kerin founded the first ADD parent workshop in Bergen County, New Jersey in 2005; she also facilitated a parents support group at the Valley Hospital in Ridgewood, New Jersey. She has also been featured in several newspaper articles. Kerin is a member of the International Dyslexia Association, International Coaching Federation, and the NJ Professional Coach Organization, and she is an affiliate of the National Speakers Association.

Kerin is also a successful entrepreneur; she is the founder of Employment Productivity, Inc. and the CEO of C.P.S. Publishing, Inc., which was founded by her father.

To learn about Kerin's upcoming lectures, teleconferences, and workshops; to inquire about hiring her as a speaker or a coach; and to sign up for her newsletter, please visit **www.ReachBeyondADD.com**.

Index

LaVergne, TN USA
05 April 2010
178149LV00001B/22/P